HAUN'
EDINBL

GW01459278

By Elena Salazar

TABLE OF CONTENTS

INTRODUCTION

In this chilling journey through the most haunted city in Scotland, we'll explore the haunted corners and eerie stories that linger amongst the gothic structures. From creepy underground vaults to mysterious castles, Edinburgh's spectral past unfolds. Join us as we delve into the ghostly whispers and lingering spirits that haunt the heart of Scotland's capital.

Edinburgh has a storied history that spans over a thousand years. The city's roots trace back to early medieval times when it was a fortress. Over the centuries, this stronghold evolved into the iconic Edinburgh Castle, perched on Castle Rock.

In the 15th century, Edinburgh became the capital of Scotland and played a crucial role in the country's political and cultural life. The city's Royal Mile, connecting the castle to the Palace of Holyrood, became the heart of its historic district.

Edinburgh experienced tumultuous times, including involvement in the Wars of Scottish Independence and conflicts with England, not to mention the bubonic plague during the 17th century.

Throughout the years, Edinburgh's architecture evolved, blending medieval, Georgian, and Victorian influences. The cityscape is characterized by narrow closes, grand squares, and iconic landmarks such as the Scott Monument and the National Museum of Scotland.

In the modern era, Edinburgh thrives as a vibrant capital, celebrated for its festivals, universities, and as a UNESCO World Heritage Site. The architecture of Edinburgh is unlike any other. It's not surprising that Edinburgh's ghost stories are as dark as the stone structures surrounding them.

WEST BOW HOUSE

There was once a neighborhood of Edinburgh known as the West Bow. Visitors may now recognize it as the area where the famous Victoria Street sits. When tourists and locals walk down the beautiful, curved, cobblestone street lined with attractive buildings and amazing shops, they may not realize that what happened here nearly 400 years ago was a scandal so horrific, it stunned an entire city.

In the late 17th century, Major Thomas Weir was known throughout Edinburgh as a distinguished covenanter soldier and devout Presbyterian, earning high regard within Edinburgh society. Known for hosting prayer sessions that attracted religious crowds, Weir's esteemed reputation led to his appointment as the commander of the Edinburgh Town Guard in 1650. By all accounts, he was perceived as an upstanding citizen until a significant shift occurred when Weir fell ill in 1670, exhibiting strange behavior.

Confined to his sickbed at the age of seventy, Weir made a startling confession, revealing a hidden life of sin and occult practices. He openly admitted to committing various grievous offenses, including bestiality, incest, necromancy, and witchcraft. Authorities, initially dismissed these claims as illusions of a sick man. However, Weir's confessions persisted, supported by corroborating admissions from his sister, Jean.

Jean added a chilling layer to the narrative, describing a demonic stranger who picked up Weir from his West Bow residence in a fiery coach. Allegedly transported to a desolate area outside of town, Weir received "supernatural intelligence" from one of Satan's minions. Jean asserted that Weir's powers were bestowed upon him through a walking stick, crowned with a carved human head, a sinister gift from the Devil himself. Eventually, the authorities took the pair's claims seriously, leading to their interrogation.

Found guilty of a litany of sinful acts, Weir and his sister faced the ultimate punishment, death. Weir met a gruesome end, being first strangled, and burned alive, along with his demonic walking stick. Rather than seeking forgiveness, Weir's reported last words were a grim acceptance of his barbaric existence.

Jean met her end through hanging in the Grassmarket. Following the executions, the Weir house on West Bow stood vacant for over a century. Locals coined the moniker "Wizard of West Bow" for Weir, speculating about the sinister events within the house. The property remained undesirable due to its rumored haunting. In the early 18th century, a courageous couple purchased the house, enduring only one night before being compelled to leave by mysterious happenings and demonic apparitions, including the sighting of a ghostly calf.

Over the years, reports persisted of strange noises, music, illuminated windows at night, and shadows moving within the rooms. Some residents even claimed sightings of a mysterious coach drawn by six fiery horses outside the house.

While it was widely believed that the Weir house was demolished in the 19th century to erase the stigma associated with it, recent discoveries in 2014 revealed that parts of Weir's house were incorporated into a new building, now known as a Quaker Meeting House. It is believed that the main part of Weir's house forms the current location of the Quaker Meeting House's restrooms. Visitors might still catch a glimpse of the Wizard of West Bow in his former home, as staff members have reported sightings of Weir's ghostly figure walking through walls, more than three-hundred years after his death, preserving the eerie legacy within the Quaker Meeting House.

THE SCOTSMAN HOTEL

Situated on North Bridge in Old Town, the former offices of The Scotsman newspaper and Edinburgh Evening News have been transformed into a luxurious 5-star hotel. Once a hub of Edinburgh's news industry, the building now houses several ghosts of its former workforce.

Among the spectral residents, a former printer from the Evening News stands out as a prominent ghost at the Scotsman Hotel. Even beyond the realm of the living, his diligent work ethic endures, with numerous sightings of his apparition tirelessly navigating the corridors and rooms.

I've stayed in this hotel twice, before I knew of it's supposed haunting, and while I never experienced anything unusual, I wouldn't want to explore alone at night. That being said, as a side note, I'd highly recommend this hotel if you're ever in Edinburgh.

HAUNTED PUBS

BANSHEE LABYRINTH

Nestled in Edinburgh's infamous South Bridge Vaults, the Banshee Labyrinth claims the title of Edinburgh's most haunted pub. The banshee, a female spirit forewarning of impending death, caused a chilling encounter when a group of workmen heard a terrifying scream. The pub also hosts a poltergeist known for violently hurling glasses across the room.

THE WHITE HART INN

Edinburgh's oldest pub, The White Hart Inn, traces back to 1516, with a rumored visit from Robert Burns in 1791. Strange occurrences, especially from the cellar, include sightings of a shadowy figure, and slamming of doors. A mischievous spirit disrupts beer taps, moves barrels, and generates loud blows and intermittent bangs in the cellar.

THE LAST DROP TAVERN

Famed for its resident ghost and linked to Grassmarket's last hanging, The Last Drop Tavern occupies a 17th-century building that once housed Edinburgh's impoverished residents. The spirit haunting the Last Drop is believed to be a young girl seen by both staff and customers in the cellar and bar area.

In the 18th century this spot hosted one of the city's primary gallows, drawing crowds for public executions. Legend has it that the pub served as the spot where condemned men enjoyed their final meal before facing the gallows outside.

TOLBOOTH TAVERN

Part of the original 16th-century Tolbooth, this tavern collected tolls and served as a Council Chamber, Police Court, and prison. Known for things being mysteriously knocked over, Tolbooth Tavern's resident ghost often takes the blame. Witnesses report drinks flying off tables and various objects falling off walls.

WHISTLEBINKIES LIVE MUSIC BAR

Built into the South Bridge Vaults, Whistlebinkies Live Music Bar harbors two ghosts – "The Imp" and "The Watcher." The mischievous Imp enjoys annoying staff, playing tricks with objects, locking people in rooms, and stopping clocks. The Watcher, a quiet spirit in 17th-century attire with long black hair, observes patrons from a distance.

DEACON BRODIE'S TAVERN

In the late 18th century, William Brodie was a highly respected figure in Edinburgh's society, known as a skilled cabinet-maker, a Town Council member, and the deacon or head of the Incorporation of Wrights and Masons. However, unbeknownst to most, Brodie secretly led a gang of burglars at night. This illicit activity was necessary to sustain his extravagant lifestyle, which included two mistresses, numerous children, and a gambling addiction.

Brodie's day job was ideal for supporting his night-time crimes, as it involved making and repairing security locks and mechanisms. He couldn't resist the temptation to copy the keys to his customers' houses, enabling him and his three accomplices to return later and steal at their leisure.

Finally, one night the thieves were caught and though Brodie, slipped away and fled to Amsterdam, he was soon apprehended and brought back to Edinburgh. A search of his house revealed tools of his illicit trade. The jury found both Brodie and one of the accomplices guilty, and their execution was scheduled for October 1, 1788.

Some say his outraged ghost lingers, frequently visiting the pub bearing his name. It is also believed that Deacon, with his double life, was the real life inspiration for Robert Louis Stevenson's Jekyll and Hyde.

BUCKINGHAM TERRACE

Buckingham Terrace represents a relatively recent addition to Edinburgh's architectural landscape, with construction commencing in the 1860s. After several years and multiple tenant changes, the Gordon Family became residents, occupying every part of the townhouse property except for a long-vacant room above them. Shortly after settling in, Mrs. Gordon was startled awake by the sounds of banging from above, resembling a physical altercation. Despite the silence that followed and her eventual return to sleep, the disturbance repeated the next night, prompting her to voice her concerns to the landlord the following morning.

Although he reassured her of the property's emptiness, the persistent noises left her unnerved, particularly when she was alone, sensing an unseen presence watching her. One night, she awoke to the sensation of this presence moving around her room, the footsteps oddly resembling hops rather than regular footsteps. Another eerie encounter occurred when the Gordons' daughter heading towards her mother's room, glimpsed the shadowy figure of a man darting past her and disappearing into the vacant room upstairs.

She decided to follow the entity and headed up the stairs. When she looked into the empty room, she saw the tall dark man shaped figure standing still as if watching her. Despite her bravery, fled once the figure began to move towards her. Following a few weeks of uneasy calm, Mrs. Gordon faced her most chilling encounter yet when her door swung open to reveal an imposing figure with distinct features—a bloody, blonde-haired man clad in an old sailor's uniform, who swiftly departed for the stairs. This harrowing event marked the Gordons' decision to hastily depart from the property.

EDINBURGH CASTLE

Perched atop Castle Rock, Edinburgh Castle has a history that spans thousands of years. Its strategic location made it a vital military stronghold and royal residence throughout the centuries.

Edinburgh Castle served as the primary residence for Scottish royalty. Queen Margaret died in the castle in 1093.

Her son, King David I, built St Margaret's Chapel in her honor, which remains the oldest building in Edinburgh and is still in use for weddings and christenings.

In 1566, Mary Queen of Scots gave birth to James VI in the Royal Palace within the castle. James VI would later unite the crowns of Scotland and England in 1603, becoming James I of England. After the Union of the Crowns, the castle was less frequently used as a royal residence and began to serve more as a military stronghold.

Today, Edinburgh Castle is one of Scotland's most iconic landmarks, attracting visitors from around the world and serving as a testament to the nation's history.

The site beneath Edinburgh Castle, predating even Jesus's time, witnessed numerous gruesome deaths throughout the centuries. Due to its dark history, Edinburgh Castle is believed to host countless spirits, leading to frequent paranormal occurrences familiar to staff and regular visitors.

When most think of ghosts of castles, they think of royals, servants, or soldiers that may have met tragic ends on the castle grounds, but two of the most famous spirits haunting Edinburgh castle were musicians. A piper and a drummer.

Centuries ago, a network of tunnels beneath the Royal Mile that led from the castle was discovered by workmen. Not knowing where the tunnel led or who had built it, the superstitious Scots selected a volunteer to investigate the tunnels. A bagpiper volunteered and said he would play his pipes along the way. As he headed off down the dark tunnel playing his pipes, people above followed the sound down the Royal Mile. His music abruptly ceased near Tron Kirk. The townspeople waited and waited for the piper to return, but he never did. Too frightened about what could have happened to him down there, a search party was never sent down and, instead, the tunnels were sealed up, forever entombing the poor piper. Visitors still report hearing the bagpipes beneath the Royal Mile.

The legend of the phantom drummer traces to 1650 where he was first spotted by a soldier that was posted on the wall of Edinburgh Castle. He heard the drumming of a single snare and went to investigate. He looked down into a courtyard and saw a boy drumming and pacing around, but to the soldier's horror, he realized that the drummer had no head! Others heard and witnessed the phantom drummer. By morning, Oliver Cromwell and his English army overtook the castle. It is believed to this day that the headless drummer was trying to warn of the approaching danger, but according to legend, the drummer is the ghost of boy that was sent by enemies to spy within the castle. Once caught, he was imprisoned in the castle dungeons and then executed by beheading. Some believe his drumming in the 1650s was a welcome to the approaching army and the spirits way of seeking justice for what was done to him within the walls of Edinburgh castle.

In the Argyll tower of Edinburgh Castle, Archibald Campbell, 9th earl of Argyll spent his last night before being executed for high treason. He was awoken the next morning, taken in a cart down to his execution site, and was beheaded. It is said that his ghost is still seen pacing about the Argyll tower.

Though Edinburgh castle was a fortified masterpiece unlike any other, it was not entirely a stronghold for its prisoners. Throughout the centuries, at least forty-nine prisoners successfully escaped from its walls, but one man's freedom was short-lived. He met a gruesome end while attempting to escape the castle's dark and damp prison. He hid in a dung barrel, hoping it would be carried out of the castle, along with his freedom. Tragically, the barrel, with the prisoner inside, was thrown over the rocky crags, leading to his death. According to some stories, this unfortunate prisoner is said to haunt the castle, attempting to push guests over the edge of the walls, seeking to make them share his fate. If you notice the foul stench of manure while walking around Edinburgh Castle, it might be wise to step away from the walls.

Perhaps the most tragic ghost haunting the medieval fortress is that of Janet Douglas or lady Glamis of Glamis castle, located in Scotland's west coast. When Janet's husband died, she was left in a vulnerable state. She belonged to the Douglas clan. Her brother had been stepfather to King James V. The

King despised him. It is thought that the King came up with a plan to punish the Douglas clan by targeting poor Janet. He seized her beloved Glamis Castle in the name of the crown and had Janet arrested. She was accused of attempted poisoning of the King and practicing witchcraft and black magic. At first she denied accusations, but before long, her son was apprehended and imprisoned, even tortured. Unable to stand the sound of her son in agony, Janet confessed. On the 17th of July, 1537, she was burnt at he stake on castle hill. After her brutal death, witnesses observed a Grey Lady, dressed in 16th century attire, weeping throughout Edinburgh Castle.

The last, and perhaps most creepy ghost haunting the castle is said to be a banshee, a female ghost that lets out a horrid bellowing shriek bringing doom to all that hear her. It is said that if she is heard, a family member will soon perish.

CANONGATE

Canongate, tracing its origins back to the 11th century, derived its name from Canon way, the route used to transport canons from Holyrood Abbey to Edinburgh Castle. Embedded within Canongate lore is the tale of a spectral figure—a young woman clad in a tartan dress — believed to have met a tragic end, stabbed by an unknown assailant in an area known as Bibleland, distinguished by a carved plaque of the Bible adorning a building's facade. One fateful night, a returning reveler ascended the stairs to his flat, only to glimpse the haunting figure of

the woman in tartan. Overwhelmed with fear, he nearly tumbled down the steps. However, his recounting of the sighting to neighbors was met with ridicule and laughter, as sightings of the apparition had become so commonplace that residents had grown accustomed to the spectral presence.

GREYFRIARS KIRKYARD

Greyfriars Kirkyard, situated in Old Town, stands out as one of Edinburgh's most haunted locations, a testament to its eerie history. Dating back to the 16th Century, Greyfriars is visited each year by paranormal enthusiasts as well as Harry Potter fans as it is said that the series author, J.K. Rowling got the inspiration for naming some of her characters from the kirkyard tombstones.

The most famous resident of the cemetery, is a little dog, affectionately known as Greyfriars Bobby. It is said that the little dog guarded the gravesite of his late, beloved owner for over a decade. There is a statue of the dog across the street from the kirkyard entrance and a pub named after the famous dog. There is even a Disney movie about Greyfriars Bobby. It is said that disembodied barking can be heard and little shadows or clouds low to the ground can be spotted by visitors to the cemetery.

One of the most famous ghosts in all of Edinburgh is known as the Mackenzie poltergeist, a restless and violent entity that comes from a time of religious unrest in Scotland. In the 17th century, King Charles II imposed strict controls on religious practices, targeting the Presbyterian Covenanters of Scotland. Despite this, many covenanters continued to hold public meetings and, before long, a small uprising was in the works.

In response, King Charles sent his son James to suppress the rebels. Leading an army of five-thousand men, James fought the rebels at Bothwell Bridge on the River Clyde. On June 22, after a long day of fighting, the covenanter rebels ran out of ammunition. The government troops then advanced unopposed, causing the rebels to flee or surrender.

George Mackenzie was the lawyer overseeing the prosecution for the captured covenanters. He had twelve-hundred of them imprisoned in a field next to Greyfriars Kirkyard, known as the Covenanters' Prison, after the Battle of Bothwell Bridge. Many were executed or died from maltreatment, earning Mackenzie the nickname "Bloody Mackenzie." Ironically, upon his death, Mackenzie was entombed in a dark mausoleum in Greyfriars Kirkyard near the Covenanters' Prison.

In 1998, a homeless man seeking shelter broke into the mausoleum. Curiosity led him to open one of the coffins, causing the floor to collapse and revealing a pit filled with decomposed bodies. Horrified, the man fled, escaping unharmed, but many believe something evil escaped that night as well. Something that had been entombed in that mausoleum for centuries waiting to be unleashed. Strange occurrences have been reported at Greyfriars Kirkyard ever since. Visitors have experienced various assaults, including bites, scratches, kicks, pushes, burns, sickness, cold forces, and even strangulation.

These events prompted the City Council to seal the mausoleum and restrict access to the covenanters prison. Now, the only way to approach the covenanters prison is through organized tours. In total, there have been over five-hundred reported attacks in the kirkyard.

EDINBURGH VAULTS, SOUTH BRIDGE

Among Edinburgh's haunted sites, the Edinburgh Vaults reign as the most popular, boasting an almost unheard-of level of reported paranormal activity. Originating in the 18th Century during Edinburgh's significant growth, these underground spaces were initially meant for legitimate businesses like taverns and cobblers. However, by 1795, flooding prompted an evacuation, leaving the vaults abandoned.

Over time, the vaults harbored illicit activities, including brothels, and became refuge for the city's poor. Rumors linked notorious serial killers Burke and Hare to the vaults, where they allegedly sought victims and stored bodies. Though unverified, the frequent paranormal occurrences suggest a history of dark dealings beneath Edinburgh.

Reports of poltergeist activity abound, particularly in a room perpetually in darkness, where any installed lightbulb would instantly explode.

Another occurrence in the vaults involves a shadowy figure known as "The Watcher" that looms in the vaults, creating an ominous presence. Visitors recount unsettling sounds; children's cries, whispered conversations, soft whimpers, and the shuffling of unseen feet in the darkness. Beyond eerie sounds, some experience the cold grasp of invisible hands and the sensation of being pulled or touched by unseen forces. A particularly malevolent spirit, possibly the Cobbler, observes women exploring the depths with mysterious intentions.

MARY KING'S CLOSE

Beneath Edinburgh's Royal Mile lies Mary King's Close, a subterranean maze of streets and dwellings where the city's poorest and most dubious residents lived until the early 1900s when it was sealed. In the 1600s, the close faced partial abandonment due to the Plague's grip on Edinburgh, with afflicted residents forced to stay, many meeting horrific deaths.

One prominent ghost in Edinburgh's folklore is the little girl haunting Mary King's Close. Perishing during the Plague in the 1600s, her spirit lingers in the home where she died, known for tugging on people's clothes and crying. According to a medium, the girl appears lonely, searching for her favorite doll. Visitors to the close sometimes leave small gifts and toys, creating a poignant connection with this spectral presence.

BORTHWICK CASTLE

Situated twelve miles southeast of Edinburgh, Borthwick Castle, dating back to the 15th century, boasts a rich history, notably serving as a refuge for Mary, Queen of Scots, in the 16th century. This well-preserved castle is not only a formidable fortress but also one of Scotland's most haunted.

Within its walls, five ghosts are said to dwell, with the most renowned being the spectral presence of Mary, Queen of Scots. Her apparition is rumored to wander the castle at night, clad in a page boy outfit—a disguise she once donned during an attempted escape from the fortress.

Another haunting tale within Borthwick Castle revolves around a lady whose ghost is said to linger in the Red Room. The tragic narrative suggests she became pregnant by one of the Lords of the castle and met a grim fate as she was stabbed and left to perish in that very room.

As one of Scotland's most haunted castles, guests staying at Borthwick have reported an unsettling sensation of being constantly watched. Some have even endured sudden and intense bouts of nausea, adding an extra layer of terror to their experiences.

DALHOUSIE CASTLE HOTEL

Situated eight miles southeast of Edinburgh, this castle-turned-luxury hotel and spa originated in the 1200s as a stronghold for the influential Ramsay family, who called it home until 1900. It proudly holds the distinction of being the oldest continuously inhabited castle in Scotland.

With its extensive history, Dalhousie Castle naturally hosts a tapestry of ghostly tales. Among them, the most prominent specter is the Grey Lady, believed to be the ghost of Lady Catherine, who met a tragic end at the age of sixteen, succumbing to a broken heart after being banished to the castle tower in 1695 for her involvement with a stable hand.

Guests staying at Dalhousie Castle often recount hearing the rustling of Lady Catherine's skirts, and some even experience a sly pinch on the neck, attributed to her ghostly presence. Interestingly, Lady Catherine appears unreserved before the

camera, frequently captured in guests'
photos, particularly during events and social
gatherings.

HOLYROOD PALACE

Nestled at the opposite end of the Royal Mile from Edinburgh Castle, the Palace of Holyroodhouse, also known as Holyrood Palace, graces Scottish Edinburgh with its rich history as the official Royal residence for the King Charles III. Situated on the castle grounds adjacent to Holyrood Palace is Holyrood Abbey, founded in 1128 by King David I.

In 1326, Robert de Bruce convened a parliament at the abbey, marking the beginning of plans to transform it into a royal residence, perhaps the most famous royal resident is Mary Queen of Scots. Upon visiting Holyrood Palace, you can catch a glimpse of what it was like back in the Renaissance age of Scotland. You can visit the Stuart Queen's chambers and look out the very windows Mary would have looked out of and imagined the absolute horrors that took place in these rooms.

Mary's second husband, Lord Darnley, was jealous of her close relationship with her private secretary and closest friend, David Rizzio. There were whispers that Rizzio had even fathered Mary's unborn child. Darnley orchestrated a plan to eliminate Rizzio and intimidate Mary, as part of a broader effort to undermine her reign.

On the evening of the 9th of March, a group of men stormed into Mary's chamber while she was dining with Rizzio. They demanded she hand him over, but she refused and tried to protect him. She was heavily pregnant the time. The men threatened her with a pistol, even aiming it at her belly. When she refused to move still, they threw her aside, and attacked Rizzio, ultimately stabbing him fifty-six times. His body was kicked down a staircase, stripped of its jewelry, and buried that night in an unmarked grave at Holyrood Abbey. Today, a grave in Canongate

Kirkyard is believed to be Rizzio's final resting place.

The murder was as much politically motivated as it was personal, yet Mary endured the assault and maintained her position as Queen. Just over a year later, in April 1567, Darnley himself was murdered, possibly with Mary's involvement, in retaliation for his role in Rizzio's assassination. But Mary seemed too frightened to have been involved as she fled Edinburgh to seek refuge with her cousin, Queen Elizabeth I, but instead of receiving asylum, Mary became a prisoner and for nineteen years she wasted away in Carlisle Castle until her execution in 1587 after being involved in an act of treason.

As for the paternity of Mary's child, later crowned King James I of England and Scotland, it remains uncertain whether he was Darnley's or Rizzio's. Contemporary sources described Rizzio as 'ugly' and 'hunchbacked,' some even state that Rizzio was believed by many at court to be a homosexual, making it unlikely that Mary would risk her reputation and marriage by engaging in an illicit relationship with him.

Visitors to the Palace of Holyroodhouse can still see the chamber where Rizzio was murdered. The supposed blood stain can even be seen on the floor. Rumor has it that no matter how many times this blood stain is scrubbed clean, the stain always reappears.

The ghost of Rizzio is seen frequently roaming about the palace. Loud thuds can be heard coming from the staircase, and the sounds of shrieking have been heard on occasion coming from Mary's bedroom.

The palace witnessed significant events, particularly during the tenure of Mary, Queen of Scots, from 1561 to 1567. Her marriage to Lord Darnley, the murder of her secretary David Rizzio, and the subsequent mysterious death of Lord Darnley in 1567 unfolded within these walls, contributing to the palace's intriguing history.

Among the reported spectral sightings, the Queen's Audience Room harbors a grey lady believed to be one of Queen Mary's ladies. Ghostly footsteps echo in the long gallery,

In 1590, King James, son of Queen Mary and Lord Darnley, was set to marry Anne of Denmark and Norway. The Danish court was highly concerned with witchcraft and black magic, which fascinated James. He traveled to to Denmark to fetch his young bride. She was just fifteen at the time and there were whispers that many at court found it to be an unsettling match. On their return voyage to Scotland, they encountered storms so severe, that James suspected witchcraft was at play. Anne's father, the King of Denmark and Norway, began interrogating women he believed were responsible for the storms.

Six women, including the wife of the mayor of Copenhagen, confessed to causing the storms to prevent Anne from leaving Scandinavia. They were burned as witches at Kronborg. Inspired by this, James established a tribunal in Scotland and took an active role, personally interrogating many accused witches. One such case was Agnes Sampson, a healer and midwife. Upon her capture, she was taken to the Palace of Holyroodhouse in Edinburgh and maintained her innocence but she was so violently tortured, she eventually confessed.

Her hair removed to find the Devil's mark, believed to be hidden under a witch's hair. After hours of extreme pain and humiliation, a mark, or more than likely, a mole or birthmark was found. Agnes confessed to witchcraft. Agnes also admitted to plotting to kill James with black magic by baptizing a cat and binding it with bones from a corpse. The bound cat was tossed into the sea creating a hex that then caused the storms that had so plagued the King and his child bride's journeys. Her confessions were, however, deemed so "miraculous and strange" that the King struggled to believe them.

She was then taken to court. When it came to her trial, it has been said that Agnes whispered to the King the very words he and his wife had shared on their wedding night which dispelled any doubts James had.

After being tried by a jury of seventeen men, many of whom would have known her personally, she was found guilty of forty-nine out of fifty-one charges, such as curing a woman who had been "bewitched by the wind" and curing another who had "walked on crutches since birth".

In 1591, she was taken to Edinburgh Castle and strangled before her body was burned at the stake. Now, some 400 years later, the ghost of the bald, beaten and naked Agnes is said to roam Holyroodhouse, the very castle where she was interrogated and forced to confess to bizarre "crimes".

In the 1990s, a young German visiting the castle claimed to have seen a bald, naked ghost approaching him. Agnes was last seen in 2014 by a maintenance man working at the palace after hours. He saw a bald, naked, and severely injured woman at the end of a well-lit corridor. The limping ghost, with her arms outstretched, approached the terrified man, who screamed as she vanished into thin air.

ROSSYLN CHAPEL

Rosslyn Chapel, commissioned in 1446 by the Earl of Orkney, is rumored to be a sanctuary for spectral entities. During a July 2006 rehearsal for an Edinburgh Festival play, actors claimed to have glimpsed fairylike figures around the chapel. One actor, upon hearing a child's voice in the crypt while locking up, ventured down to find no one there.

Legends tell of a white lady's ghost haunting Rosslyn Castle, bewitched and awaiting rescue by a knight to break the spell. Ghostly apparitions, including a phantom dog with eerie barking on stormy nights, are said to roam the chapel's grounds. Monks, thought never to have left, reportedly pray in the crypt, with sightings of one surrounded by knights.

Mysterious noises and a chilling wind near the crypt entrance add to the chapel's enigma. In 2010, uneasy workmen shared experiences of feeling watched, and one encountered a monk while repairing crypt steps. Despite skepticism, these tales contribute to the enduring mystique of Rosslyn Chapel, leaving one to ponder if it holds more than mere memories.

CHESSEL'S COURT

Chessel's court is a beautiful area of Edinburgh consisting of numerous elegant houses built in the 1740s. It's best known as the setting for Robert Louis Stevenson's Jekyll and Hyde, but it is just as famous for the many sightings of the notorious lady in black.

One dark winter evening in the late 18th century, a resident named Mrs. Gordon, was sitting down by the fire reading when she heard the faintest sound a person outside her door. She slowly made her way over and pressed her ear to the door. She could hear the sound of heavy breathing just outside her door. Though it sounded frightening, she realized that she lived up several flights of stairs and anyone could be out of breath from the climb so she ignored it.

But this happened night after night and finally, one night, when she heard the heavy breathing outside her door, she worked up the courage flung the door open. There was no one outside her door and the breathing stopped. She looked around the room and on the ceiling. Had the breathing been coming from inside her home all along? Terrified, she went straight to bed and tried to put the whole thing out of her mind. She decided she was going to ignore it all from that moment on. She became accustomed to hearing the breathing. So much so, that when her brother paid a visit several months later, she didn't even think to tell him about the ghostly visitor.

After retiring for the night and falling asleep, Mr. Gordon awoke to a feeling of unease. He quickly stroked a match and, to his horror, he saw the dark silhouette of a woman, tall and frail. The match went out. When another was lit, the apparition had disappeared. Mr. Gordon fled the house, never to return.

It is thought that the specter is the spirit of a young woman that had lived in the house back in its glory days before it was split up into flats and was a big beautiful mansion. It is said that she suffered from depression and one day, in a fit of despair, she hanged herself the room that Mr. Gordon had spotted her in.

In 1985, a tenant had woken up to get a glass of water. After getting back into bed, he heard the landlords dog growling and trying to get into his flat. Suddenly, a dark figure came out of the wall and started to climb over him. He could feel the spirit pushing down on the blankets. He was in such a state of shock, he did not move until the ordeal was over.

As we conclude our journey through the haunted corners of Edinburgh, it's undeniable that this city's history is steeped in tales of the supernatural. From the echoing chambers of the South Bridge Vaults to the mysterious apparitions at Edinburgh Castle, Edinburgh stands as a testament to the lingering spirits of centuries past.

Whether you believe in spirits or not, Edinburgh remains a city of captivating tales, where the past and the paranormal intertwine, leaving an indelible mark on those who dare to explore its shadowy realms. As we bid farewell to the ghostly secrets hidden within its stone walls, remember that the spirits of Edinburgh may still have untold stories waiting to be unveiled in the depths of the night.

Printed in Great Britain
by Amazon